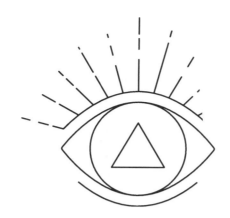

3 **6** **9**

"IF ONLY YOU KNOW THE MAGNIFICENCE OF 3, 6 AND 9 THEN YOU WOULD HAVE THE KEY TO THE UNIVERSE"

NIKOLA TESLA

Nikola Tesla was a Serbian-American inventor, electrical engineer and physicist born in 1856. He played a crucial role in the development of alternating current (AC) electrical systems. Tesla held numerous patents for his inventions, including the induction motor and the Tesla induction motor and the Tesla coil. He worked with Thomas Edison before parting ways over the AC versus DC power battle. Tesla's contributions to science also include pioneering work in radio waves and wireless communication. Despite his groundbreaking work, Tesla struggled financially in his later years and died in relative obscurity in 1943. Today, he is recognized as one of history's most influential inventors and his ideas continue to impact various fields, including electricity, robotics, and wireless technologies.

What is the 369 theory of Tesla?

According to Tesla , 3 , 6 and 9 are the only numbers that can exist as Energy without losing their identity. This concept is supported by modern physics , Which recognizes the importance of these numbers in the study of atomic and subatomic particles.

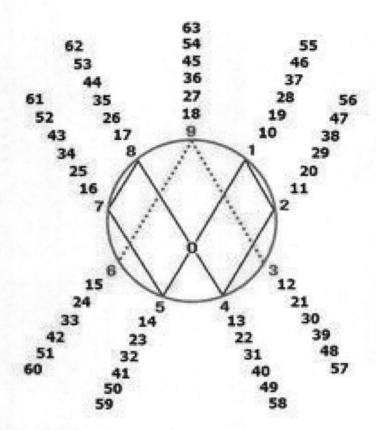

How 369 manifestation method works?

The method involves writing down your desired manifestation three times in the morning, six times during the day, and nine times in the evening. This repetition throughout the day is believed to reinforce your intention and signal the universe to bring your desire into reality.

WRITE

WANT

ASK

WISH

IMAGINE

VISUALIZE

GET

CONCRETE

THANKS

"Write your manifestation down three times in the morning, six times in the afternoon and nine times in the evening."

Speak to your subconsciousness, which is your direct connection to the universe and your dreams come true!

Desire : to get a big salary
Emotions : gratitude, love, integrity
Affirmation : I am so grateful that my salary is so much more important, my future will be amazing.
Thanks, UNIVERSE

How to use the 369 METHOD in daily life?

" It is essential to maintain a positive attitude, to embrace the present moment and to avoid using phrases that are grounded in negative words. Additionally it is necessary to visualize what one desires and to experience the associated emotions."

"During your creation, simply focus your thoughts on something positive that you deeply desire. Avoid the company of negative, envious or inquisitive individuals with ulterior motives. This moment is precious it is your creation and no negative influence should interfere. Safeguarding your dreams and creations should be at your discretion. If you feel the need to share them, choose to do it, so only with people who genuinely love you, devoid of jealousy and who can envision your success."

"Surround yourself with positive people WHO DOESN'T JUDGE YOU and motivates you in your projects."

"For example, if you dream of becoming an elementary school teacher, share it with a friend or a family member who can envision you positively in that role, rather than with someone who might internally doubt your abilities and hinder the realization of your creation."

"WRITE **3** TIMES"
AT PRESENT
YOUR WISH

"WRITE **6** TIMES"
YOUR
INTENTION

"WRITE **9** TIMES"
THE ACTION THAT
YOU WISH TO
ACHIEVE

EXAMPLE: You dream of a significant promotion for the coming year.

Write down this desire **3 times**, being as specific as possible, Include details about salary, position, relocation, etc.

Then, write down **6 times** the feelings you would experience upon achieving this promotion.

Finally, write down **9 times** in the evening, preferably shortly before bedtime. It is crucial to vividly visualize yourself in the situation of obtaining your promotion, including the surroundings, the place and how you would celebrate it. For instance, envision celebrating joyfully at a restaurant surrounded by your loved ones and family. These three numbers are not arbitrary.

1. I am currently achieving my dream promotion, envisioning the specific details of the position, salary and positive changes it brings to my career. **(3 TIMES/MORNING)**

2. In my visualization, I see myself in my desired role, confidently handling responsibilities, and enjoying the increased recognition and respect from my colleagues. **(6 TIMES/AFTERNOON)**

3. As I celebrate my successful visualization, I am surrounded by supportive colleagues and family, relishing the joyous moment of accomplishment, perhaps at a celebratory dinner or gathering. I feel a profound sense of achievement and fulfillment. **(9 TIMES/EVENING)**

3 = DESIRE
6 = IMAGINATION & SENSATION
9 = MANIFESTATION

The key to the success of the 369 method lies in consistency, determination, precision and attention to detail during the imagination process.

NEVER DOUBT !

it's the trap! This feeling is negative. Be extremely vigilant and unwavering. Only individuals with good self-esteem succeed.

For example: You perform a task and if you don't complete it correctly, you might naturally say to yourself, "Oh, I'm foolish," or "Oh, I'm worthless." Avoid such statements all your self-talk should be positive !

Writing is an extension of yourself. Believe in YOURSELF. You write, you imagine, you achieve, you manifest...

"If your imagination is challenging, it's important to practice.
Engage in visualization exercises using images and photos that you cut out and paste into your visualization journal.
Visualize this journal before bedtime, describing aloud what you see.
For example: you cut out and paste image of your dream car, a house and a watch. 'I envision myself in my new 120m2 house with a garden, terrace and garage, where my new [brand] car, colored red, is parked. I sit behind the wheel with my new [brand] watch on my wrist.' Be specific as that is the key and feel the emotions associated with it."

1 _____
_____
_____
_____

2 _____
_____
_____
_____

3 _____
_____
_____
_____

1

2

3

4

5

6

1

2

3

4

5

6

7

8

9

1 _____

_____

_____

_____

2 _____

_____

_____

3 _____

_____

_____

1

2

3

4

5

6

1

2

3

4

5

6

7

8

9

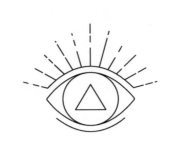

1 _____

_____

_____

_____

2 _____

_____

_____

_____

3 _____

_____

_____

1

2

3

4

5

6

1

2

3

4

5

6

7

8

9

1 _____

_____

_____

_____

2 _____

_____

_____

3 _____

_____

_____

1

2

3

4

5

6

1

2

3

4

5

6

7

8

9

1 _____

_____

_____

_____

2 _____

_____

_____

_____

3 _____

_____

_____

1

_____

_____

_____

2

_____

_____

_____

3

_____

_____

_____

4

_____

_____

_____

5

_____

_____

_____

6

_____

_____

_____

1

2

3

4

5

6

7

8

9

1
_____

_____

_____

_____

2
_____

_____

_____

3
_____

_____

_____

1

2

3

4

5

6

1

2

3

4

5

6

7

8

9

1
_____
_____
_____
_____

2
_____
_____
_____

3
_____
_____
_____

1

2

3

4

5

6

1

2

3

4

5

6

7

8

9

1 _____

_____

_____

_____

2 _____

_____

_____

_____

3 _____

_____

_____

1

2

3

4

5

6

1

2

3

4

5

6

7

8

9

1

2

3

1

_____

_____

2

_____

_____

3

_____

_____

4

_____

_____

5

_____

_____

6

_____

_____

1

2

3

4

5

6

7

8

9

1 _____

_____

_____

_____

2 _____

_____

_____

_____

3 _____

_____

_____

1 _____

_____

_____

2 _____

_____

_____

3 _____

_____

_____

4 _____

_____

_____

5 _____

_____

_____

6 _____

_____

_____

1

2

3

4

5

6

7

8

9

1 _____

2 _____

3 _____

1

2

3

4

5

6

1

2

3

4

5

6

7

8

9

1
_____

_____

_____

_____

2
_____

_____

_____

_____

3
_____

_____

_____

1

2

3

4

5

6

1

2

3

4

5

6

7

8

9

1
_____
_____
_____
_____

2
_____
_____
_____

3
_____
_____
_____

1

2

3

4

5

6

1

2

3

4

5

6

7

8

9

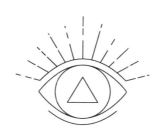

1
_____

_____

_____

_____

2
_____

_____

_____

3
_____

_____

_____

1

2

3

4

5

6

1

2

3

4

5

6

7

8

9

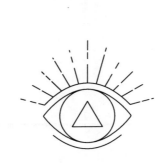

1 _____
_____
_____
_____

2 _____
_____
_____
_____

3 _____
_____
_____

1

2

3

4

5

6

1

2

3

4

5

6

7

8

9

1 _____

_____

_____

_____

2 _____

_____

_____

3 _____

_____

_____

1

2

3

4

5

6

1

2

3

4

5

6

7

8

9

1

2

3

1

2

3

4

5

6

1

2

3

4

5

6

7

8

9

1 _____

_____

_____

_____

2 _____

_____

_____

_____

3 _____

_____

_____

1

2

3

4

5

6

1

_____

_____

2

_____

_____

3

_____

_____

4

_____

_____

5

_____

_____

6

_____

_____

7

_____

_____

8

_____

_____

9

_____

1

2

3

1

2

3

4

5

6

1

_____

2

_____

3

_____

4

_____

5

_____

6

_____

7

_____

8

_____

9

_____

1
_____

_____

_____

_____

2
_____

_____

_____

3
_____

_____

_____

1

2

3

4

5

6

1 _____

_____

2 _____

_____

3 _____

_____

4 _____

_____

5 _____

_____

6 _____

_____

7 _____

_____

8 _____

_____

9 _____

_____

1
_____

_____

_____

_____

2
_____

_____

_____

_____

3
_____

_____

_____

1

2

3

4

5

6

1

2

3

4

5

6

7

8

9

1 _____

_____

_____

_____

2 _____

_____

_____

_____

3 _____

_____

_____

1

2

3

4

5

6

1

2

3

4

5

6

7

8

9

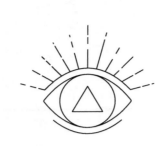

1
_____
_____
_____
_____

2
_____
_____
_____

3
_____
_____
_____

1

2

3

4

5

6

1

2

3

4

5

6

7

8

9

1 _____

_____

_____

_____

2 _____

_____

_____

_____

3 _____

_____

_____

1

2

3

4

5

6

1
_____

_____

2
_____

_____

3
_____

_____

4
_____

_____

5
_____

_____

6
_____

_____

7
_____

_____

8
_____

_____

9
_____

_____

1
_____
_____
_____
_____

2
_____
_____
_____
_____

3
_____
_____
_____

1

2

3

4

5

6

1

2

3

4

5

6

7

8

9

1 _____

_____

_____

2 _____

_____

_____

3 _____

_____

_____

1

2

3

4

5

6

1

2

3

4

5

6

7

8

9

1 _____

_____

_____

_____

2 _____

_____

_____

3 _____

_____

_____

1

2

3

4

5

6

1

2

3

4

5

6

7

8

9

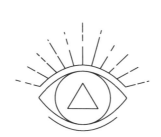

1
_____

_____

_____

_____

2
_____

_____

_____

_____

3
_____

_____

_____

1

2

3

4

5

6

1

2

3

4

5

6

7

8

9

1

2

3

1

_____

_____

_____

2

_____

_____

_____

3

_____

_____

_____

4

_____

_____

_____

5

_____

_____

_____

6

_____

_____

1

2

3

4

5

6

7

8

9

1 _____

_____

_____

_____

2 _____

_____

_____

_____

3 _____

_____

_____

1

2

3

4

5

6

1

2

3

4

5

6

7

8

9

VISION BOARD

A vision board is essentially a physical (or digital) manifestation of your goals. Vision boarding involves collecting images or objects that speak to the future you want to create and arranging them on a board for a tangible and aesthetically pleasing reminder of where you're heading

What is the power of a visualization board?

But it's not just a board with pictures and words, it's an inspirational, motivational, aspirational tool to push you towards your goals, dreams, aspirations over the next 12 months. The timeframe is deliberate: it focuses the mind and makes the goals much more achievable.

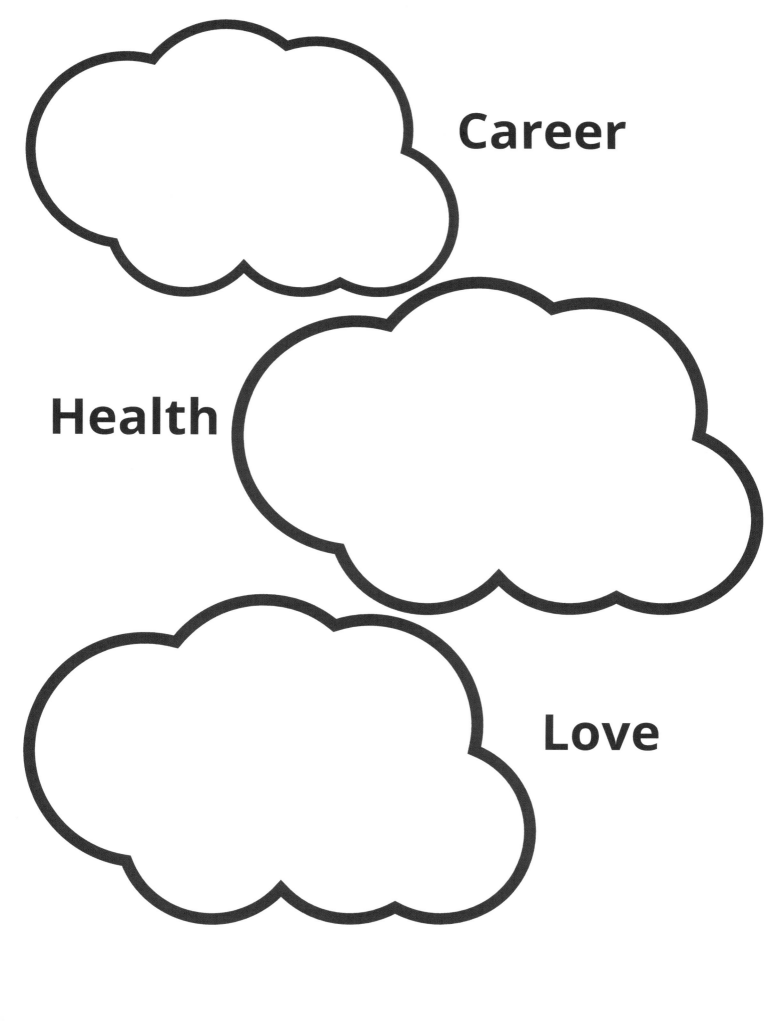

Career

Health

Love

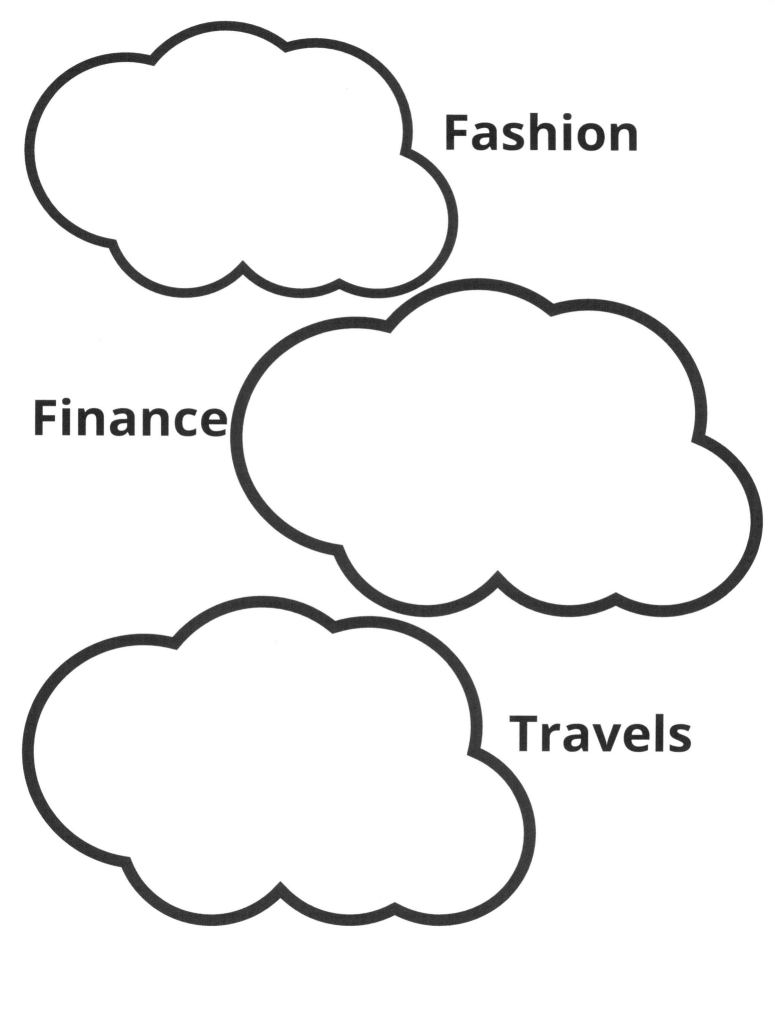

Fashion

Finance

Travels

Home

Mindset

Goals

"Don't be afraid
be Focused, be determined, be hopeful,
be empowered !"
....
Michelle Obama

"Thank you so much for
accompanying me throughout
this journey. Your valuable time
and interest are priceless gifts. To
all the readers, I extend my
deepest gratitude."
....
Linda Carter

Made in United States
Troutdale, OR
05/26/2024